Olmec, Mayan, Aztec

Kimberley Sorensen

www.Steck-Vaughn.com
1-800-531-5015

The Lost American Empires: Olmec, Mayan, Aztec
By Kimberley Sorensen

Photo Acknowledgements
Cover ©Thom Lang/CORBIS; p. 9 ©Sven Martson/The Image Works; p. 11 ©Macduff Everton/CORBIS; p. 13 ©Werner Forman/Art Resource, NY; p. 15 ©The Art Archive/Antochiw Collection Mexico/Mireille Vautier; p. 15 ©Yann Arthus-Bertrand/CORBIS; p. 17 ©Owen Franken/CORBIS; p. 19 ©Sean Sprague/The Image Works; p. 20 ©Charles & Josette Lenars/CORBIS; p. 23 ©Karl Kummels/SuperStock; p. 24–25 ©The Art Archive/Museo Ciudad Mexico/Dagli Orti; p. 27 ©The Granger Collection, New York; p. 29 ©Topham/The Image Works.

Additional Photography by Royalty-Free/CORBIS

ISBN 1-4190-2290-3

© 2007 Harcourt Achieve Inc.

All rights reserved. No part of the material protected by this copyright may be reproduced or utilized in any form or by any means, in whole or in part, without permission in writing from the copyright owner. Requests for permission should be mailed to: Paralegal Department, 6277 Sea Harbor Drive, Orlando, FL 32887.

Steck-Vaughn is a trademark of Harcourt Achieve Inc.

Printed in the United States of America
1 2 3 4 5 6 7 8 152 12 11 10 09 08 07 06 05

TABLE OF CONTENTS

Introduction
A New World?............................ 4

1 The Olmecs
Whose Head Is It, Anyway?............. 8
Play Ball! 14

2 The Maya
Can Too Much Sun
Destroy a Civilization?................ 16
Sacred Mountains..................... 22

3 The Aztecs
How Did a Few Hundred
Soldiers Conquer an Empire?.......... 24

Glossary 30
Index 32

INTRODUCTION

A NEW WORLD?

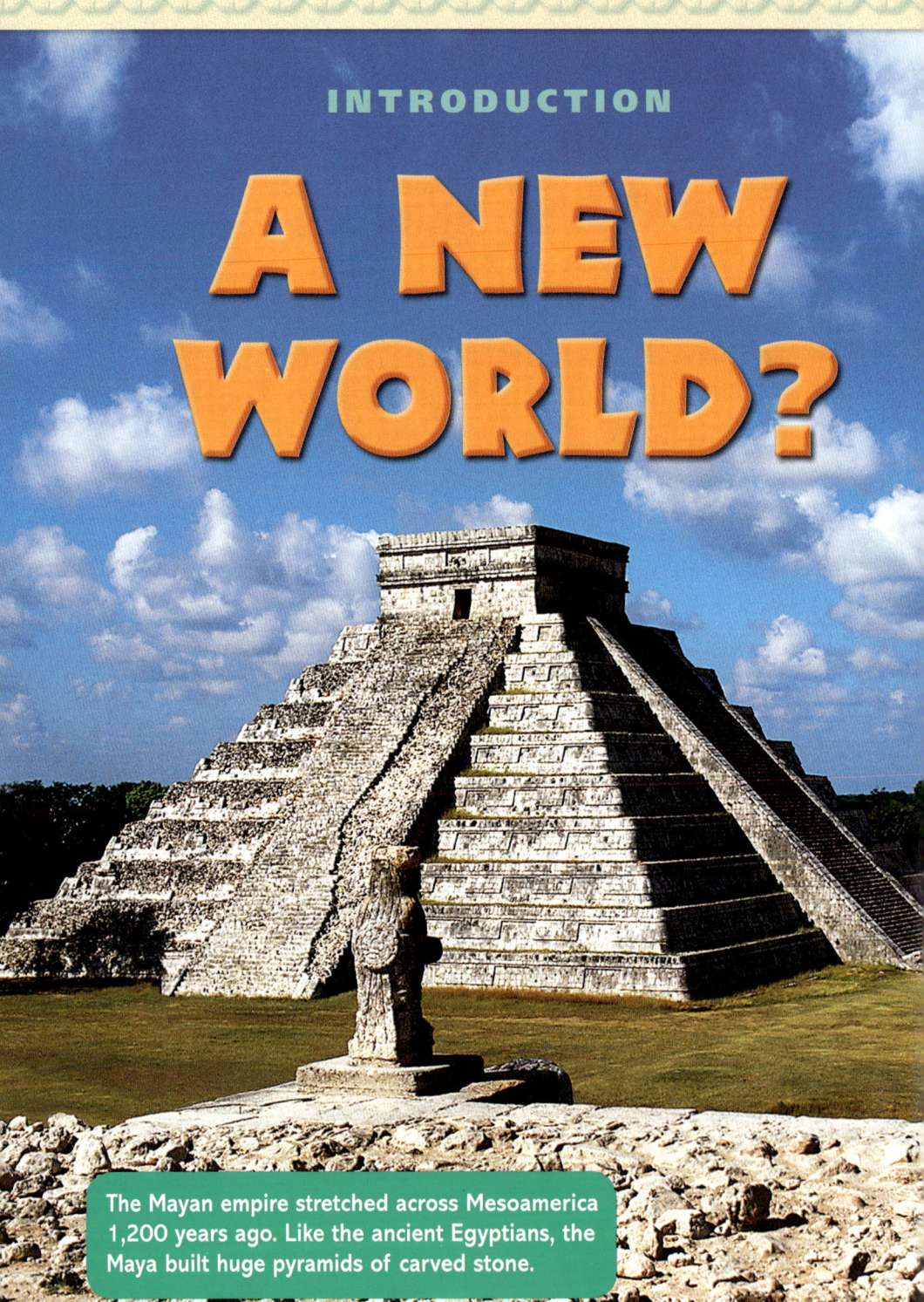

The Mayan empire stretched across Mesoamerica 1,200 years ago. Like the ancient Egyptians, the Maya built huge pyramids of carved stone.

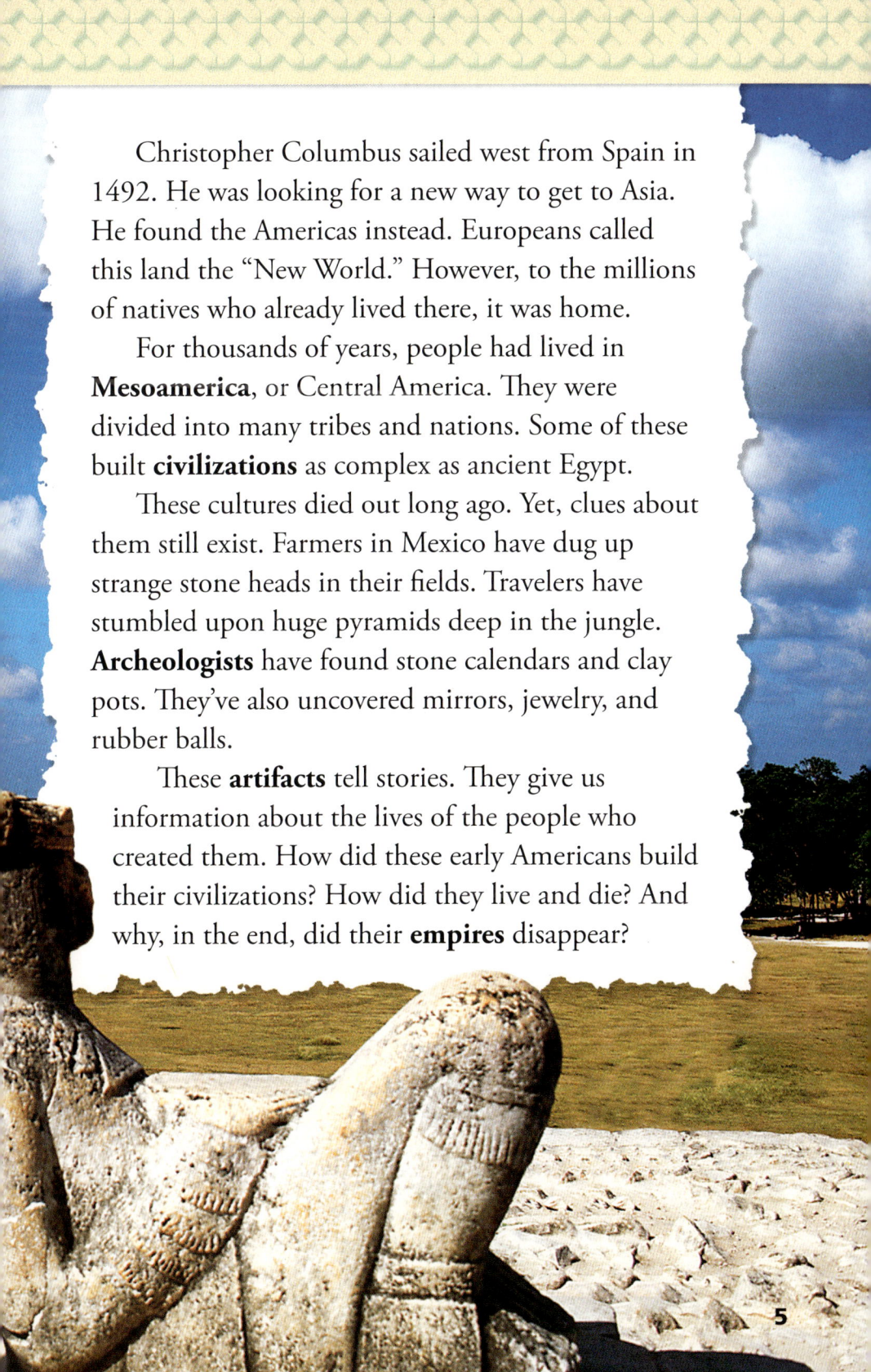

Christopher Columbus sailed west from Spain in 1492. He was looking for a new way to get to Asia. He found the Americas instead. Europeans called this land the "New World." However, to the millions of natives who already lived there, it was home.

For thousands of years, people had lived in **Mesoamerica**, or Central America. They were divided into many tribes and nations. Some of these built **civilizations** as complex as ancient Egypt.

These cultures died out long ago. Yet, clues about them still exist. Farmers in Mexico have dug up strange stone heads in their fields. Travelers have stumbled upon huge pyramids deep in the jungle. **Archeologists** have found stone calendars and clay pots. They've also uncovered mirrors, jewelry, and rubber balls.

These **artifacts** tell stories. They give us information about the lives of the people who created them. How did these early Americans build their civilizations? How did they live and die? And why, in the end, did their **empires** disappear?

The Mesoamerican Map

About 3,500 years ago, civilization began to emerge in Mesoamerica. People learned to harvest corn in large amounts. The corn gave them a reliable food supply. With plenty of food available, they were free to do other things. Some people had time to carve jewelry and sculptures. Others built large monuments. The first American civilization was born.

Olmec

The Olmecs formed the first true civilization in the area. They were scattered across swampy valleys near the Gulf of Mexico. Around 1500 B.C., they began to build towns. They also began to carve huge heads from volcanic rock. In the end, these sculptures were lost under centuries of dirt. But why had the Olmecs carved these heads?

Mayan

The Mayan people lived to the south and east of the Olmecs. Around A.D. 300, they started to build cities, too. They constructed huge pyramids. They learned to write. They studied the stars and used a calendar. Then, by A.D. 1000, many of their cities were empty. Why did the advanced Mayan culture disappear so suddenly?

Aztec

The Aztecs came to central Mexico around A.D. 1200. They conquered much of Mesoamerica. Then, in 1519, the Spanish arrived. They had only a small army. The Aztecs numbered in the millions. Still, in two short years, the Aztecs were defeated. How did it happen?

These are the mysteries of Mesoamerica.

CHAPTER 1

THE OLMECS
Whose Head Is It, Anyway?

One morning in 1862, a farmer was at work in his fields in southern Mexico. His shovel hit something hard. At first he thought he had found an old pot. The deeper he dug, however, the bigger the object got.

After hours of digging, the farmer stood back. He was amazed. He had uncovered a huge stone head. It stood 5 feet tall and weighed 8,000 pounds. Where had it come from? Who was it supposed to be? Who had made it, and why?

No one on the planet knew the answer. The people who had carved the head had been gone for centuries. No one knew who they were or what they were called.

So for the next 80 years, nobody did much about the mysterious head.

Eventually, 17 giant heads were found. Most Olmec sculptures show people with flat faces like the one shown here. ▶

Heads Up

Finally, in the 1930s, archaeologists got curious. They traveled to the area where the first head was found. Farmers told them about a huge stone eye. It peered up from a jungle path. Others showed them small carvings made of **jade**. The farmers had found these tiny objects in their fields.

The archaeologists began digging. Within a few years, they had found sixteen more giant heads. Some of them were more than nine feet tall and weighed forty tons.

These discoveries raised new questions. Some archeologists said the heads' features looked African. Others said that they looked Asian. Still others **assumed** that the heads had been carved by Mayan or Aztec people. However, the heads were 3,000 years old. That was much older than the Maya or the Aztecs. So, who could have made them?

There were other questions, too. The stones had been moved at least fifty miles from their original location. With no trucks or cranes, how could these people have moved the stones so far? Why would they go to the trouble?

Slowly, the archaeologists uncovered clues about the makers of the heads. The heads were found in an area full of rubber trees. In the Aztec language, "Olmec" means "people of the rubber country." So, archaeologists called the people the Olmecs.

The Olmecs, they found, practiced **agriculture**. To clear space for fields, they chopped down trees and bushes. Then, they burned the remains. This practice is called slash-and-burn farming.

After the trees were burned, the ashes **fertilized** the soil for three to five years. During this time, the Olmecs farmed the land. Once the land became **infertile**, they had to find a new place to plant crops.

At some point, Olmec farmers made an important discovery. Like the Egyptians, they found that land along a river stayed fertile. Every time the river flooded, mud fertilized the soil. Unlike slash-and-burn farmers, riverside farmers didn't need to move to find good soil. This discovery allowed people to settle down. The size of their communities grew.

The Olmecs' most important crop was a wild grass called maize, or corn. The maize grew easily. One bushel of seed produced 100 bushels of corn.

A 20th-century Mayan farmer sits near his harvest of corn. The Olmecs produced a similar harvest 3,500 years ago.

The size of the harvest was important to the Olmecs. The large food supply allowed them to spend less time farming. They had more time for other activities. They learned how to make pottery. They traded it all across Mesoamerica. In exchange, they received beautiful feathers. They also traded for blue and green jade. Olmec artists carved the hard jade into sculptures.

Sacred Stone

The huge heads, though, were different. They were made out of tons of volcanic rock. Yet, there were no volcanoes within fifty miles of any Olmec city. How did the Olmecs move the heavy rocks?

Archeologists believe that they made ropes out of vines. The Olmecs used the ropes to drag the rocks to the river. Then, they tied the stones onto huge rafts. They floated the stones downriver to the cities.

That leaves a more important question. Why would the Olmecs go to so much trouble for a hunk of stone? The answer may lie in several large stone thrones found along with the heads. The thrones and heads were probably carved for Olmec rulers. Some of the thrones show a ruler climbing up from below the earth.

What does it mean? Some archeologists have a theory. They think the Olmecs believed in a **sacred**

This throne shows an Olmec ruler rising from the underworld. It's carved from volcanic rock.

area beneath the earth. Volcanoes led into this sacred space. To the Olmecs, volcanic rock was like a gift. It would have been very valuable to them.

When rulers died, the Olmecs may have recarved their thrones. Perhaps they transformed the thrones into the giant heads. The heads would have honored the rulers. In this way, many generations would remember the rulers.

Later, as the Olmec civilization declined, the heads were damaged and buried. Why? That question is still a mystery.

PLAY BALL!

In 1989, archaeologists found an Olmec treasure. They dug up a burial site that contained offerings the Olmecs had made to their gods. Among them were a couple of rubber balls the size of volleyballs.

The discovery surprised archeologists. The area where the Olmecs lived was hot and humid. The climate wasn't like the dry heat of Egypt. In Egypt, things like pottery, cloth, and paper could last for thousands of years. In the Olmec homeland, moisture rotted most artifacts. Only stone and jade and pottery survived over the years.

Somehow, these balls survived. Archaeologists were excited by the find. The balls proved that the Olmecs played a sacred game known throughout the Americas.

The game took skill. Players tried to knock the ball into a goal made from a large, stone hoop. They could use their hips, knees, and elbows. They couldn't use their hands or feet.

It was a fast, rough game. And it paid to win. Sometimes the winners got to take jewelry and clothes from people in the audience. Sometimes the losers may have been killed.

The game may be part of a Mesoamerican creation story. This story tells how the world began.

The Maya also played the sacred game. It may have been the first team sport ever played.

Twin brothers went into the underworld. There, they played the game with the gods. They lost. The gods killed them, but the brothers came back to life. They challenged the gods again. This time, the twins won. As a reward, the gods made a new Earth for them. It was the world of Mesoamerica.

CHAPTER 2

THE MAYA

Can Too Much Sun Destroy a Civilization?

The first Spanish explorers reached central Mexico about 500 years ago. There, they met people who called themselves Maya. The Maya lived in small huts. The huts were simple. Yet, what the Spanish found in the backyards was not.

Many of these huts were built near the ruins of huge stone cities. The Spanish had never seen cities like these. To the villagers, the crumbling buildings were no big deal. The ruins were old. The people who had built them were forgotten.

In fact, the villagers' Mayan **ancestors** had built those cities. More than a thousand years earlier, in A.D. 800, the ancient Maya ruled a huge empire. It stretched across Central America and southern Mexico. It was a busy, wealthy civilization. It may have held 500 people per square mile. The streets of the great Mayan cities would have been as crowded as many large cities of today.

This hut is probably much like the ones the ancient Maya lived in. When they died, they were buried under the floor of their hut. That way, they could communicate with the underworld.

Mayan civilization had a lot in common with ancient Egypt. Both civilizations grew their food near rivers. Both had strong leaders. Both built huge cities and pyramids from stone. Both used hieroglyphics, a kind of picture writing.

There was at least one big difference between the Egyptians and the Maya. The Egyptian empire lasted for more than 3,100 years. The Mayan empire fell apart after 650 years. Why did this great empire die out?

Expert Farmers

The ancient Mayan civilization was on the eastern third of Mesoamerica. It was very mountainous, and the area wasn't good for farming. They didn't have large animals to pull plows.

Even so, the Maya became excellent farmers. They made the best of what they had. They built **terraces** in the hillsides. Terraces are strips of flat land where crops can be planted. They also drained their swamps. Then, they built raised fields in marshy areas. They knew it was smart to weed their fields so that their crops could grow as strong as possible. This is something Europeans didn't do at the time. These practices **illustrate** the advanced culture and civilization of the Mayan people.

For food, the Maya planted a wide variety of crops. They grew tomatoes and beans. They grew squash, peppers, and corn. They even made chewing gum from the sap of the sapodilla tree.

The Maya also noticed which plants grew well together. Corn stalks made good poles for bean plants to climb. Squash grew well in the shade of the corn and beans. Their big leaves helped keep the ground cool and moist.

Different kinds of food grew better in some places than in others. That meant trade was important. People from one village traded food and goods with people from other villages.

The cacao bean grows in pods on a tree trunk. It's used to make chocolate. The cacao tree was common in Mesoamerica. The ancient Maya used its beans as a form of money.

The Maya were probably excellent walkers. They had to be. They had no horses or oxen to carry them. They built paved roads called **causeways** to walk on. The causeways were two to four feet above ground and had trees for shade. The Maya even built rest houses along the way. People from the closest villages made sure the rest houses had food and firewood.

The Maya also built enormous pyramids and **observatories**. There, they could watch the movements of the stars and planets. They made calendars based on what they saw. Just like the calendars of today, the Mayan calendar counted 365 days per solar year.

The Maya did a lot to make their empire great. By A.D. 800, they had a **population** of millions. The people lived in hundreds of cities and towns. Some cities controlled the villages around them. Yet, no city had **authority** over all the others. There was no president or king who ruled the entire empire.

Deadly Dry Spells?

The city rulers fought among themselves for power. Neighboring Mayan tribes battled each other fairly often. So, did war destroy the great cities of the Maya? That's part of the reason. It doesn't explain it all, though.

Scientists have now uncovered a more powerful enemy. That enemy was the weather. **Geologists** studied the layers of mud and rock found under the water sources in the region. Those layers told them which years had a lot of rain and which were dry.

They found that the Maya suffered through three long **droughts**. The dry spells came between A.D. 810 and 910. Each lasted almost ten years. Day after day the sun beat down. The soil grew dry and cracked.

Even the Maya couldn't farm without water. Their farmers couldn't produce enough to support the cities. Their food supplies ran out, along with their drinking water. Some cities were conquered by new rulers. Others were simply deserted. The people moved to smaller villages. The huge, empty cities gradually fell into ruin. Before long, no one was left to remember the glory of the Maya.

◀ This Mayan observatory served the city Chichén Itzá. It was designed very carefully. Its windows directly face the sun and the planet Venus on certain days of the year.

SACRED MOUNTAINS

Imagine that you wake up and find yourself in an ancient city. A huge stone pyramid rises in front of you. Where would you be, in Ancient Egypt or Mesoamerica? How could you tell the difference?

Look at the pyramids. Do they have steps up the front? If so, you'd probably be in Mesoamerica. Plus, you'd be looking at an important clue to the way the Maya worshipped. To the Maya, the steps weren't just a way to get a nice view. They were probably considered a pathway to heaven.

The Maya believed that people lived in the middle of the universe. Below lay the underground world of water. Above hung the heavens of the birds and the stars. Any place where these worlds came together was sacred. Mountains and birds were sacred. They brought heaven and Earth together. Volcanoes and deep lakes were sacred, too. They brought together Earth and the underworld.

To the Maya, pyramids were sacred mountains. They were arranged by the position of the sun and stars. Astronomers observed the sky from the pyramids. They charted the stars and the planets. Mayan priests used the information to predict events.

Tikal was one of the biggest Mayan cities. Its Great Plaza was surrounded by huge stone pyramids. They still stand today.

Would the harvest be plentiful? Is it a good day for battle? They thought the stars held the answers.

Sometimes, the Maya buried their dead in the bottom of pyramids. The Egyptians did the same. The most important part of the Mayan pyramid, though, is found at the top. It was the "god house." Only priests were allowed to climb to the sacred place.

CHAPTER 3

THE AZTECS

How Did a Few Hundred Soldiers Conquer an Empire?

In 1519, Spanish explorer Hernando Cortés led 400 Spanish soldiers into the island city of Tenochtitlán. Later, one of the soldiers wrote about the city. "Everything was shining and decorated with stonework and paintings," the soldier wrote. He remembered the sweet smells of the gardens. He recalled the songs of the birds. "I thought that no land like it would ever be discovered in the whole world." It was bigger than most cities in Europe. Nearly 200,000 people lived there.

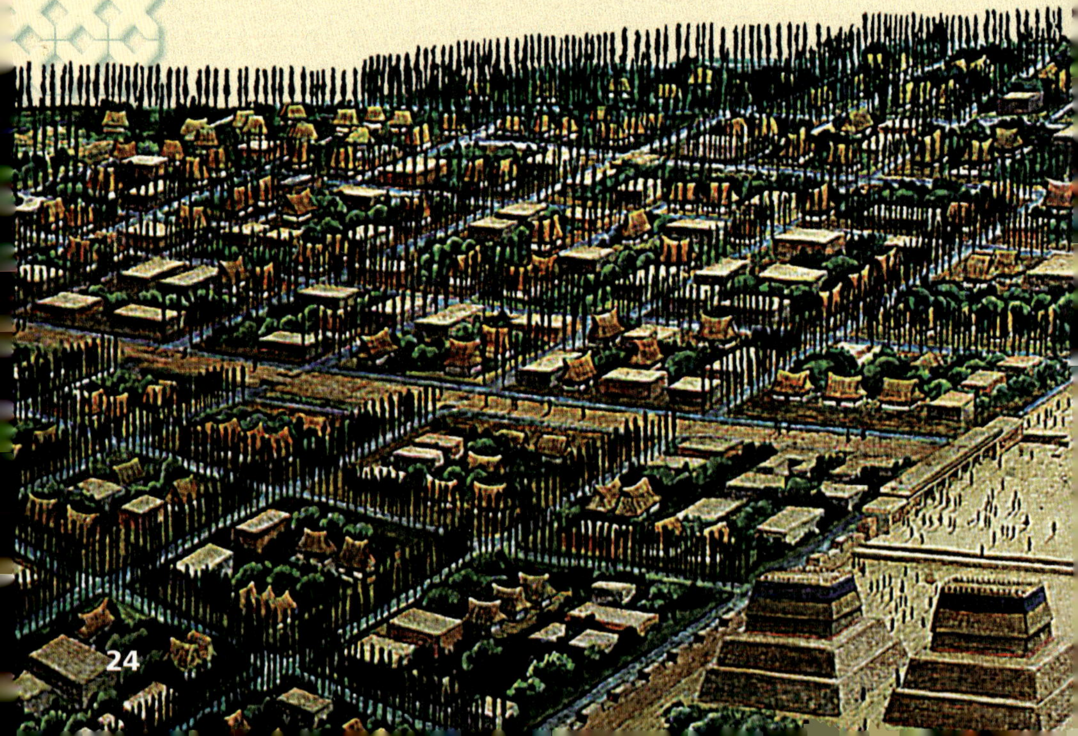

The soldier sadly added, "But today all that I then saw is overthrown and destroyed. Nothing is left standing." The city was in ruins. The dead bodies of Aztec men and women lined the streets. Their books had been burned. Their art had been destroyed. In two short years, Spanish soldiers had nearly erased the history of the Aztecs.

How could such a great civilization fall apart so quickly?

The Spanish arrived in Tenochtitlán in 1519. The Aztecs welcomed Cortes with a great ceremony. They thought he was Quetzalcoatl, a light-skinned god that they had been expecting. According to legend, Quetzalcoatl had taught the Aztecs about both farming and government.

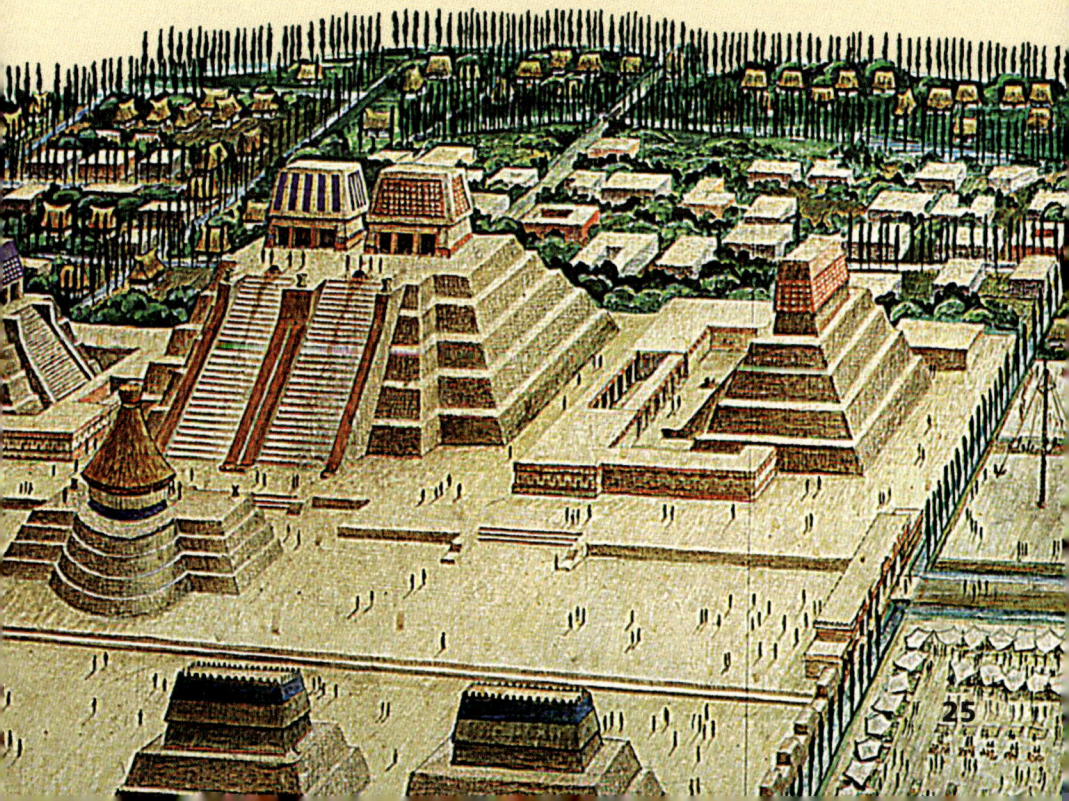

Rise of the Aztecs

Aztec civilization rose almost as quickly as it fell. The Aztecs came to central Mexico around A.D. 1200. They were searching for a new home. Legend has it that their holy men told them to look for a sign. "Home will be where an eagle sits on a cactus holding a snake."

The Aztecs found the eagle on an island. The island sat in the middle of Lake Texcoco. The Aztecs didn't let that stop them. They built a city on the island and called it Tenochtitlán. In time, they needed more farmland. So they made their own islands. They wove rafts together and heaped mud on them. These mud islands were called ***chinampas***.

The Aztecs were fearless warriors. They thought their gods would reward them for a brave death. Their most important god was Huitzilopochtli. Each night, he fought with darkness to bring back the sun. The Aztecs believed he needed blood to stay strong.

Aztec warriors conquered many tribes. The defeated tribes were forced to send gifts to their Aztec rulers. These gifts were called **tributes**. The tribes also sent slaves. Some of these slaves were sacrificed to Huitzilopochtli.

The Aztecs fought to defend Tenochtitlán, but the Spanish had better weapons. They also enlisted the help of the Aztecs' enemies.

The Secret Weapon

The Aztecs were powerful warriors. They had conquered millions of people. Their empire stretched for hundreds of miles. They outnumbered the Spanish troops. How did Cortes defeat them?

First of all, the Spanish had better weapons and armor. The Aztecs fought mainly with clubs. The Spanish fought with guns. The Aztecs protected themselves with clothing made of cotton. The Spanish wore metal armor.

The Spanish also had help from the Aztecs' neighbors. Other tribes hated and feared the Aztecs. Many of them helped the Spanish soldiers.

One weapon was more powerful than all the rest. And the Spanish didn't even know they had it. They carried germs with them from Europe. The germs caused smallpox, measles, and whooping cough. Europeans had lived with these diseases for a long time. Their bodies knew how to fight them.

To the Aztecs, these illnesses were new. They were unknown to the rest of Mesoamerica, too. The germs spread over hundreds of miles. By 1620, ninety percent of Mesoamerica's native population was dead. Most of them had been killed by these strange, new diseases.

Mesoamerican Mysteries

The Olmec, Mayan, and Aztec empires are gone. Yet buildings, artwork, and writings remain. These artifacts fascinate both tourists and scientists. Each year, millions of people go in search of these ancient civilizations. Visitors travel all over Central America. They marvel at the ancient sites. Meanwhile, archeologists uncover more lost treasures. They study the artifacts and search for answers. Little by little, they piece together the history of Mesoamerica.

This Aztec sun stone was carved in the 1400s. It is twelve feet across and weighs almost 25 tons. It acted as a calendar. The stone shows how the Aztecs thought the world began. It also shows how they thought it would end. According to the calendar, Quetzalcoatl would return in 1519. He would destroy the Aztec empire. Cortes arrived that year.

GLOSSARY

agriculture *(noun)* the production of crops and raising of livestock

ancestor *(noun)* a relative who lived a long time ago

archeologist *(noun)* a scientist who studies the past by digging up old buildings and objects

artifact *(noun)* something made or used by human beings in the past

assume *(verb)* to think or suppose something is true without checking it

authority *(noun)* the power to tell other people what to do

causeway *(noun)* a raised roadway

chinampa *(noun)* an island made from rafts and mud

civilization *(noun)* a highly advanced and organized society

drought *(noun)* a long period of time without rain

empire *(noun)* a large territory or group of countries led by one ruler

fertilize *(verb)* to make soil rich for growing plants

geologist *(noun)* a scientist who studies the earth's layers of rock

illustrate *(verb)* to explain by demonstrating or showing an example

infertile *(adjective)* not able to grow crops or plants

jade *(noun)* a green stone used for carving and making jewelry

Mesoamerica *(noun)* the region extending from central Mexico to Costa Rica

observatory *(noun)* a building from which to watch the night sky

population *(noun)* the total number of people living in an area

sacred *(adjective)* holy; having to do with religion

terrace *(noun)* flat ground carved out of a slope

tribute *(noun)* a gift or payment made to show loyalty or thanks

Idioms

no big deal *(page 16)* not special or important
Since we moved to Alaska, going snowboarding is no big deal.

INDEX

agriculture, 10–12, 18–20, 21, 26
artifacts, 5, 6, 28
authority, 20
Aztecs, 7, 10, 24–29

balls, 5, 14–15

calendars, 5, 6, 20
causeways, 20
cities, 6, 12, 16, 18, 20, 21, 24, 26
civilizations, 5, 6, 16, 18, 24, 26, 29
Columbus, Christopher, 5
corn, 6, 10, 19
Cortés, Hernando, 24, 27
cultures, 5, 6, 18

diseases, 28–29
droughts, 21

Egypt, 5, 14, 18, 22, 23
empires, 16, 18, 20, 24, 27

fertile land, 11

jade, 10, 12, 14

maize, 10
Maya, 6, 8, 10, 16, 18–23
Mesoamerica, 5, 6–7, 14–15, 22, 29

observatories, 20, 22
Olmecs, 6, 8, 10–15

population, 16, 20, 29
pyramids, 5, 6, 18, 20, 22–23

sculptures, 5, 6, 8, 10–13
Spanish explorers and soldiers, 5, 7, 16, 24, 27–29

Tenochtitlán, 24, 26
terraces, 18
trade, 12, 19
tributes, 26

volcanoes, 6, 12, 13, 22

writing, 6, 18, 28

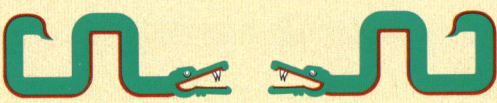